SPORTS ZONE

BASKETBALL
A Guide for Players and Fans

BY HEATHER WILLIAMS

CAPSTONE PRESS
a capstone imprint

Fact Finders Books are published by Capstone
1710 Roe Crest Drive, North Mankato, Minnesota 56003
www.capstonepub.com

Editorial Credits
Lauren Dupuis-Perez, editor; Sara Radka, designer;
Eric Gohl, media researcher; Laura Manthe, production specialist

Photo Credits
Flickr: Miami University Libraries, 17; Getty Images: Christian
Petersen, 20, Erik Isakson, 27, Kyle Terada, 4, Photodisc, 29 (bottom),
South_agency, cover (background), Tobiaz Titz, 10-11 (court);
Newscom: Brian Rothmuller/Icon Sportswire DHZ, 16, David
Santiago/TNS, 18, EFE/Mike Brown, 23, Icon Sports Media, 12,
TNS/Hector Amezcua, 24, UPI/Jon Soohoo, cover (foreground);
Pixabay: intographics, bkgd; Shutterstock: Aspen Photo, 11 (players),
Billion Photos, 8-9, emka74, 13, emregologlu.com, 14, OSTILL is
Franck Camhi, 10 (player), pedalist, 28, Salajean, 29 (top); Wikimedia:
Unknown, 6, 7, Verpacker Ing., 25

Library of Congress Cataloging-in-Publication Data
Names: Williams, Heather, 1974- author.
Title: Basketball: a guide for players and fans / by Heather Williams.
Description: North Mankato, Minnesota: Capstone Press, [2019] |
Series: Fact finders. Sports zone | Audience: Ages: 8 to 9. | Audience:
Grades: K to grade 3.
Identifiers: LCCN 2019005977 | ISBN 9781543573565 (hardcover) |
ISBN 9781543574555 (pbk.) | ISBN 9781543573688 (ebook PDF)
Subjects: LCSH: Basketball–Juvenile literature.
Classification: LCC GV885.1 .W545 2019 | DDC 796.323–dc23
LC record available at https://lccn.loc.gov/2019005977

TABLE OF CONTENTS

INTRODUCTION

Basketball is a high-scoring game. In 10 seasons with the Golden State Warriors, Stephen Curry has scored more than 15,000 points.

The buzzer sounds in Quicken Loans Arena in Cleveland, Ohio. The Golden State Warriors have won the 2018 National Basketball Association (NBA) championship. It is their third championship in four years. They could not have done it without point guard Stephen Curry. He is one of the best players in the NBA today.

After high school Curry was not offered a scholarship to play for any big college teams. They thought Curry was too short at 6 feet, 3 inches (190.5 centimeters). He chose to play at Davidson College, a small college in North Carolina. Curry turned out to be one of the best players in college basketball. He joined the Golden State Warriors in 2009. Curry has helped Golden State become a championship team and one of the greatest teams in NBA history.

Teams like the Warriors and great players like Curry make basketball a favorite sport in the United States. More than 26 million people play basketball in the United States. Only a few will get to play pro basketball like Steph Curry. However, it is a sport that many people can enjoy watching and playing.

championship—a contest or tournament that decides which team is the best

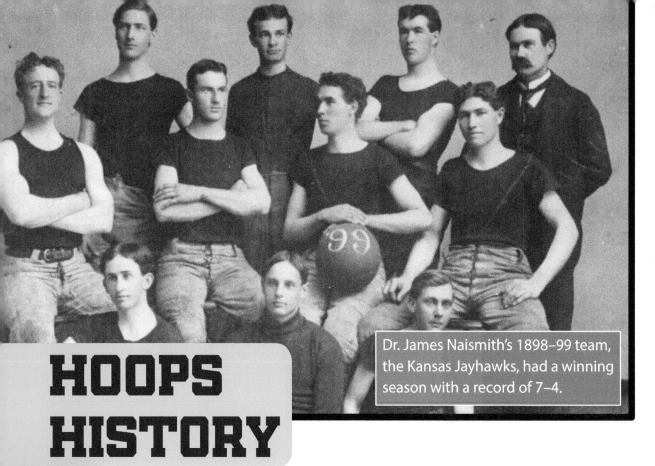

Dr. James Naismith's 1898–99 team, the Kansas Jayhawks, had a winning season with a record of 7–4.

HOOPS HISTORY

It was a snowy winter in Springfield, Massachusetts. The year was 1891. Teacher and coach Dr. James Naismith was teaching a physical education class. It was too cold to go outside. The students were bored and needed an indoor game to play. Naismith thought about a game he and his friends had played as kids. He asked a janitor to hang two peach baskets up in the gym. He gave his students a soccer ball and a few rules. Basketball was born.

The students loved Naismith's new game. He made up 13 rules. A magazine published the rules so people everywhere could play the game. Under these rules, players could pass the ball or bat it with their hands. At that time there was no **dribbling**. Basketball quickly spread to schools and community centers across the United States. A few colleges started basketball clubs. Smith College started the first women's basketball team in 1893.

After inventing basketball, Dr. James Naismith coached the sport.

Naismith went to work at the University of Kansas in 1898. He started the first college basketball team there. Today Kansas is still known for its winning basketball program. In 1936, basketball became a sport at the Olympic Games. Naismith was there. He was a very old man by then. The United States won the first gold medal for basketball. Naismith handed out the medals.

dribbling—bouncing a basketball off the floor using one hand

From the start basketball spread quickly across the United States. Basketball was becoming one of the most popular sports at most colleges and universities. Schools like Indiana University, Duke University, the University of Kentucky, and the University of California, Los Angeles, became famous for their basketball teams.

The first professional teams were formed in 1898. The Basketball Association of America (BAA) began in 1946. It became the National Basketball Association three years later. The Women's National Basketball Association (WNBA) began in 1996.

That same year the Olympics let professional basketball players play in the Olympic Games for the first time. Michael Jordan of the Chicago Bulls was one of those players. The United States won Olympic gold. Everyone around the world loved watching Jordan play. He helped make basketball an international game. Jordan is still a big name in basketball today.

1891

1895

1936

1939

1946

Dr. James Naismith creates a game that came to be known as basketball. He publishes his 13 rules of the game in January 1892.

The first game of basketball is played between two colleges, Hamline College and the Minnesota State School of Agriculture.

Basketball becomes an Olympic sport. Dr. Naismith throws up the ball to start the first game.

The first NCAA basketball tournament takes place between eight college teams. Oregon beats Ohio State to win the first college national championship.

The Basketball Association of America is founded. Three years later the BAA becomes the National Basketball Association, or the NBA.

The New York Renaissance

One of the greatest basketball teams of all time was the New York Renaissance. The team was founded in 1923. They were the first African American professional basketball team in the United States. The Renaissance played about 3,000 games from 1923 to 1949. They won more than 2,000 of them. Three of the team's star players made history as the first black players in the NBA in 1950.

FACT

The Harlem Globetrotters were not based in Harlem, New York. They started in 1927 in Chicago, Illinois, and didn't play a game in Harlem until 1968.

GEAR FOR THE GAME

Not much equipment was needed to play the very first game of basketball. This is still true today. A ball and a hoop are the only things needed to start a game. The first basketball was made in 1894 by A.G. Spalding & Bros. It was brown. Basketballs were not orange until the late 1950s. The first basketball goal was a peach basket. There was a small hole in the bottom of the basket. When a basket was scored, a person who worked at the gym poked the ball out with a long stick. Dr. James Naismith added **backboards** so fans on the second floor could not block the net or take the ball during games.

backboard—a glass rectangle behind the hoop and net

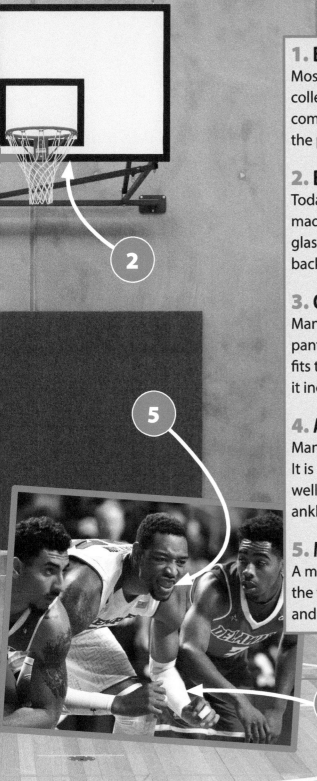

1. Ball

Most basketballs are made of rubber. NBA and college basketballs are made from leather. They come in different sizes based on the ages of the players.

2. Basket and backboard

Today's baskets have metal rims with nets made of thick string or steel. Wood and glass were used to make some of the first backboards. Today most are made of Plexiglas.

3. Compression clothing

Many players wear compression sleeves and pants when they play. Compression clothing fits tightly around the body. Some studies show it increases blood flow and can decrease injury.

4. Athletic shoes

Many basketball players wear high-top shoes. It is important to get basketball shoes that fit well, keep the feet in place, and prevent the ankles from turning.

5. Mouthguard

A mouthguard is a piece of rubber that fits over the teeth. Mouthguards protect players' teeth and tongues during games.

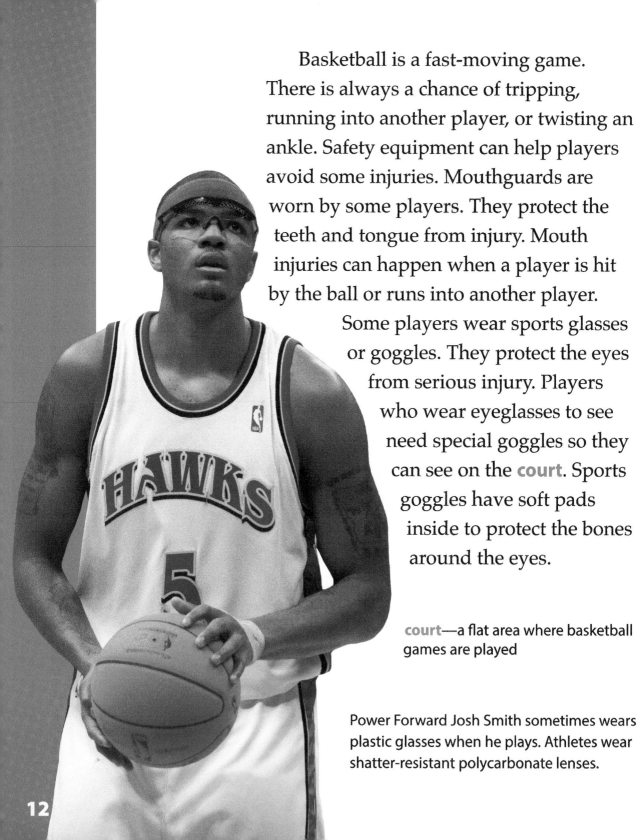

Basketball is a fast-moving game. There is always a chance of tripping, running into another player, or twisting an ankle. Safety equipment can help players avoid some injuries. Mouthguards are worn by some players. They protect the teeth and tongue from injury. Mouth injuries can happen when a player is hit by the ball or runs into another player.

Some players wear sports glasses or goggles. They protect the eyes from serious injury. Players who wear eyeglasses to see need special goggles so they can see on the **court**. Sports goggles have soft pads inside to protect the bones around the eyes.

court—a flat area where basketball games are played

Power Forward Josh Smith sometimes wears plastic glasses when he plays. Athletes wear shatter-resistant polycarbonate lenses.

Knee and ankle injuries are common in basketball. Knee and elbow pads can protect the joints in case of falls. Joint pads are most common in youth basketball. Many older players and professional players wear knee and ankle braces. They provide extra support and protection for players who have already injured a knee or ankle.

Shoes are the most important piece of equipment for basketball safety. The first basketball shoes were made in 1917. They were high-tops made by Converse. High-tops provide extra ankle support, but basketball shoes can also be low-top. Good basketball shoes should support the feet and keep them from twisting or sliding around. A good pair of shoes can help prevent ankle and knee injuries.

FACT

Converse Chuck Taylor shoes only came in high-tops until 1962. Colors other than black and white were not made until 1966.

BASIC RULES

A three-point shot is made at least 22 feet (6.7 meters) away from the basket.

A regular basketball court is 94 feet (29 meters) long and 50 feet (15 m) wide. Court sizes are smaller for younger players. Every court has a mid-court line halfway between the two goals. At each goal is a basket and a backboard. The maximum basket height is 10 feet (3 m). Youth teams have lower baskets.

A basketball game has four **quarters** at most levels. There is a halftime period between the second and third quarters. The length of each quarter is based on the league that is playing. For example, NBA quarters are 12 minutes long. In high school the quarters are eight minutes long. Youth quarters can be as short as five minutes each. Women's college games have four 10-minute quarters. Men's college games have two 20-minute halves instead of four quarters.

quarter—one fourth of a game; in the NBA, one quarter is 12 minutes

Early basketball games were played with nine people on each team. The number of players changed to five in 1897. Today all teams play five players at a time, from youth all the way up to the NBA. The five traditional positions on a basketball team are the center, small forward, power forward, shooting guard, and point guard.

Centers are usually the tallest players on the court. They are often good at blocking shots. Small forwards can play all over the court, defending near the basket and on the outside. Power forwards may also be good scorers, but they must be able to **rebound** the ball. Shooting guards are hard to cover. They are often the best shooters on the team and may be a bit taller than the point guard. Point guards are like coaches on the court. Their main job is to help their team run plays and score a basket. The point guard is usually the quickest player on a team. They should be skilled at passing and dribbling.

rebound—to gain possession of the ball after a missed shot

Boban Marjanović of the Los Angeles Clippers is the tallest player in the NBA, at 7 feet, 3 inches (221 cm) tall.

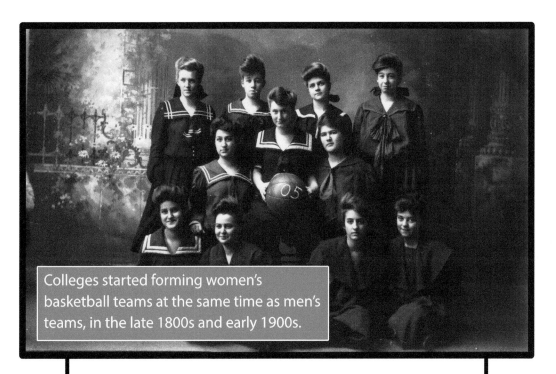

Colleges started forming women's basketball teams at the same time as men's teams, in the late 1800s and early 1900s.

Women's Basketball History

Women started playing basketball not long after it was invented. However, the rules for women were very different at first. Women were only allowed to play on half the court. They also had to wear dresses. They were always expected to be proper. They were not allowed to shout or sit on the floor. Today women play professional basketball and mostly play by the same rules as men.

During his NBA career, from 2007 to 2017, Luis Scola (right) averaged 2.7 personal fouls per game.

When basketball was brand-new there were only 13 rules. There are many more rules today, and they are very important. Some rules help players stay safe. Others keep the game moving.

If the ball or the player holding the ball goes out of bounds, the other team gets to throw the ball back into the game. Players cannot pick up the ball and walk with it. This is called traveling. They must dribble it down the court with one hand. Bouncing the ball with both hands at the same time is called a double dribble and is not allowed. Teams in college have up to 30 seconds to take a shot. In the NBA teams only have 24 seconds. If a player hasn't taken a shot in the allotted time, the other team gets the ball.

Even though basketball is action-packed, it is not a contact sport. Players cannot hit, trip, or shove each other. These are called fouls. If a player fouls a shooter in the process of taking a shot, the shooter is allowed to take free throw shots.

FACT

Before 1923, one player on the team took all the free throw shots during a game. A new rule that year required players to take their own free throws when they were fouled.

out of bounds—outside the playing area

BASKETBALL STRATEGY

Diana Taurasi (3) is a three-time WNBA Champion and a four-time Olympic gold medalist in basketball. She has played for the Phoenix Mercury for her entire pro basketball career.

Basketball teams have two main jobs. The most important job of a team is to score lots of points. The team's other job is to stop the other team from scoring. When a team is trying to score it is called offense. When a team is trying to stop the other team from scoring it is called defense.

Each player has a job on offense and a different job on defense. Power forwards and centers are in charge of defensive rebounds. This means they try to get to the ball first after the other team shoots. Still, every player on the floor must rebound for a team to have success. Each player is also charged with guarding the opposing team. The goal is to stay between the opposing players and the basket without fouling to make scoring difficult.

Defense

Offense is fun to watch, but good defense usually wins out. A winning team makes sure the other team scores fewer points than they do. There are two basic types of defense in basketball. One is called zone defense. The other is called man-to-man defense.

Zone defense means that each player covers an area of the court when the other team has the ball. Players in a zone defense keep pressure on any opponent who enters that area. Defenders try to cut off passes into their area and put pressure on ball-handlers who come their way.

Man-to-man defense is when each player guards one player from the other team. In man-to-man defense, players stick to the player they are guarding like glue. This makes it harder for the other team's players to take shots. Some teams use a mix of zone and man-to-man.

When playing defense, players are allowed to put their hands, arms, and bodies in the way of the opposing player.

Manu Ginobili drives to the basket for a short-range shot to score against the Dallas Mavericks.

Offense

Scoring is one of the most fun parts of basketball. All offensive plays are meant to get the ball past the defense and into the hoops. During an offensive possession, players often try to block the path of a defender so someone can get open to take a shot. This is called setting a screen. A speedy player can also beat the other team down the court and shoot. This is called a fast break.

One key to a good offense is passing. Quickly moving the ball around the court creates space between the offense and defense. Keeping spaces open on the court creates chances for scoring. When players dribble too much or try to pass in crowded spaces, defenders can easily steal the ball. Longer passes keep the ball moving and make the defense work harder.

Players can score with layups, dunks, free throws, and jump shots. Layups and dunks are taken right under the rim of the hoop. A dunk is when a player jumps up and slams the ball into the basket. Most jump shots are taken outside the **lane**. These shots are worth two points. A free throw shot is worth one point. A jump shot taken outside the three-point arc is worth three points.

lane—the dark, rectangle-shaped area in front of the basket

Even though not everyone can become the next Stephen Curry, anyone can learn to play and enjoy basketball. The only way to get better is to get out and play the game. Learning the basics, such as dribbling and shooting, is important. Starting **pickup** games, in a park or gym can be a good way to learn skills. Older players can help younger players work on their skills.

It is also important to be active. Running, exercising, and playing other sports help the body become more athletic. This is called cross-training. Eating well is important too. The world's top athletes eat plenty of fruits and vegetables every day. Drinking lots of water also helps the body work properly.

pickup—a type of game that is played just for fun

More than 15 million Americans play pickup basketball. Worldwide it is one of the most popular sports.

Finding a Team

One of the best ways to enjoy basketball is to join a youth team. Most schools have team sports like basketball starting in sixth or seventh grade. Many elementary schools have basketball clubs after school. If there's no team or club at a school, maybe it is just waiting for the right player to come along and start one!

There are community basketball teams in almost every city and town. City parks and recreation departments have youth and adult teams. Some churches have sports programs that include basketball. Kids can even sign up for a team at the local YMCA, where basketball started so many years ago. Communities have teams for kids as young as 5 years old! No one is too young or old to enjoy one of the most popular sports in the United States.

The NBA recommends that kids interested in basketball try other sports too, then focus on basketball at 14 years old.

FACT

More than half of kids ages 6 to 12 in the United States play in a team sport. Around 4 million of them are on a basketball team.

Kids who stay active and play sports can have up to 40 percent higher test scores.

Getting Involved in Team Sports

Playing a team sport has many benefits. Being part of a team helps kids stay healthy. Getting exercise and practicing a sport every day builds strong muscles and healthy bones. Teams also help build lasting friendships. Playing a sport gives young athletes a way to deal with stress. Spending time with friends and working toward a common goal together can help kids cope with the pressures of life and school.

Glossary

backboard *(BAK-bord)*—a glass rectangle behind the hoop and net

championship *(CHAM-pee-uhn-ship)*—a contest or tournament that decides which team is the best

court *(KORT)*—a flat area where basketball games are played

dribbling *(DRIB-ling)*—bouncing a basketball off the floor using one hand

lane *(LAYN)*—the dark, rectangle-shaped area in front of the basket

out of bounds *(OWT OV BOWNDS)*—outside the playing area

pickup *(PIK-up)*—a type of game that is played just for fun

quarter *(KWOR-tur)*—one fourth of a game; in the NBA, one quarter is 12 minutes

rebound *(REE-bound)*—to gain possession of the ball after a missed shot

Read More

Bryant, Howard. *Legends: The Best Players, Games, and Teams in Basketball.* New York: Philomel Books, 2017.

Chandler, Matt. *Wacky Basketball Trivia: Fun Facts for Every Fan.* Wacky Sports Trivia. North Mankato, MN: Capstone, 2017.

McCollum, Sean. *Basketball's Best and Worst: A Guide to the Game's Good, Bad, and Ugly.* The Best and Worst of Sports. North Mankato, MN: Capstone, 2018.

Schaller, Bob. *The Everything Kids' Basketball Book:* The All-time Greats, Legendary Teams, Today's Superstars—and Tips on Playing like *a Pro.* New York: Adams Media, 2017.

Internet Sites

The Naismith Memorial Basketball Hall Of Fame
www.hoophall.com

Jr. NBA
jr.nba.com

Sports Illustrated Kids: Basketball
www.sikids.com/basketball

Index